Surrender

A SEVEN-DAY DEVOTIONAL

Stacy Smartt Pelotshweu

SLA
SIGHT LITERARY AGENCY

surrender

a. (*verb*) to yield to the power, control, or possession of another upon compulsion or demand

b. (*verb*) to give up completely or agree to forgo,
especially in favor of another

— Merriam-Webster's Dictionary

Foreword

There are books that teach, books that inspire, and then there are those rare gems that do both, while also transforming the reader. This devotional is one of them.

We were deeply moved by Stacy's transparency and sensitivity to the Holy Spirit. Each story, scripture, and prayer is woven together with divine intention, offering not only encouragement but also a clear call to action: to let go and let God be God in every area of your life. We've had the joy of walking closely with her and have witnessed firsthand her integrity, deep faith, and unwavering pursuit of God, even through life's hardest seasons. Her life is a living testimony of the very surrender she so beautifully writes about

The message of surrender is timeless, yet more urgent than ever. In a world that champions self-reliance, this devotional courageously calls us back to the sacred rhythm of trusting God not in part, but completely. It gently confronts, lovingly corrects, and beautifully affirms the heart that dares to yield. And in doing so, it reminds us that true victory is not in striving, but in surrender.

From the very first page, it is evident that Stacy has not written from a theoretical perspective, but from the trenches of lived experience, where faith is tested, hearts are broken, and hope is reborn through surrender. These pages are soaked in honesty and rich with revelation.

To the reader: Take your time with this book. Don't rush through the days. Let each devotion breathe over you like healing rain. Let it minister to the hidden places. We pray that as you walk through this seven-day journey, you will discover the nearness of God in new ways and encounter the peace that only surrender can bring.

Drs. Jerry & Jana Lackey
Founders Lackey Ministries
Love Botswana Outreach Ministry

CONTENTS

Introduction

I surrender all, I surrender all;
all to Thee my blessed Savior, I surrender all.

For over a century, Judson W. DeVenter's 1896 hymn "All to Jesus I Surrender" has called us to give everything to Jesus. "I surrender all" sounds sweet when set to a tune, but it is quite challenging to put into practice. Why does God ask us to surrender?

Because we cannot deal with life's hardships on our own.

Life is challenging. Whether we live in luxury or lack, we will all experience moments of joy and sadness, victory and defeat, health and sickness. As children of God, we are not exempted from difficulties; in fact, Jesus said in John 16:33, "In this world you will have trouble." Challenges, or as the Bible calls it, "trouble," can come from different sources in our lives: relationships, career/work, finances, health, or just the uncertainty and fear of the unknown. A traumatic event or an unrestrained thought can produce feelings of frustration, anger, anxiety, or worry. Our inability to cope with life's challenges can cause emotional, physical, or mental strain.

If we do not manage our responses to life's challenges, disappointments will make us susceptible to the enemy's lies, subsequently altering our personalities. For years, my responses to life's challenges were far from godly, and my faith, relationships, and sense of identity all suffered because of it.

When I was a teenager, my father left our family. My mother was devastated, and I felt embittered. My father's betrayal made me believe that I could not rely on anyone, not even God. As I grew older, I vowed never to put myself in a vulnerable position where I felt helpless. I was intentional about becoming self-reliant and remaining in control of all aspects of my life. I built a wall around my heart and learned to love with reservations. This worked for a while, but what I did not know was that there was a cost to being in control. I was under immense pressure, constantly evaluating my decisions and anticipating the outcomes. Anxious and fearful of what could go wrong, I became inflexible and self-centered. To prevent myself from experiencing the hurt I witnessed my mother endure, I was unconsciously mimicking my father's actions.

My life changed when I learned to surrender.

We do not have to live anxious, worried lives or allow ourselves to be driven by the things we fear most. God has made a provision—a way for us to manage our responses to life's challenges. He invites us to simply cast our cares on him. Learning to surrender all things to God has redefined my life and given me peace that surpasses my understanding. In John 16:33, Jesus concludes by saying "Take heart! I have overcome the world." God has allotted to us the same overcoming grace, and boy, do we need it.

*"My life changed when I
learned to surrender."*

This devotional came out of a difficult period in my life, from dealing with issues of abandonment to raising children, relocating, and navigating all of life's challenges. For seven days, God woke me up every morning and directed me to a different area of my life to surrender to him. This devotional covers these seven areas, along with biblical stories, a scriptural invitation that reveals the promises of God and His expectations of us, a call to action, and a prayer. I am sharing this with you because I believe this will benefit us all. Though our lives may differ, the principles and benefits of a surrendered life remain the same.

As you begin this devotional, I encourage you to commit to the seven-day journey. Do not break the seven-day rhythm. In the Bible, the number seven has great significance—seven speaks of completion, covenant promises, divine intervention, and rest. God rested on the seventh day of creation (Genesis 1), the walls of Jericho fell on the seventh day (Joshua 6), and in the book of Revelation, there is mention of seven letters to the seven churches, seven seals, seven trumpets, and seven bowls.

My prayer is that in the next seven days, God will reveal everything that hinders you from surrendering all. And that you will replace the enemy's lies with the truth of God's word.

> "For the word of God is living and active and full of power [making it operative, energizing, and effective]. It is sharper than any two-edged sword, penetrating as far as the division of the soul and spirit [the completeness of a person], and of both joints and marrow [the deepest parts of our nature], exposing and judging the very thoughts and intentions of the heart."
>
> — Hebrews 4:12 AMP

Surrender

DEVOTION

Human beings resist surrender. Often, the word *surrender* is associated with defeat or giving up, which does not sound appealing. But surrender is not complete in merely giving up. True surrender begins with giving up, but it ends with giving over.

One day, God showed me the power of surrender in the simplest way. Because of my busyness, I decided to give my eleven-month-old baby a bath in the sink instead of the tub. I am not sure why I thought that was a good idea, but it certainly was strange for my little one. The unfamiliar shape and slippery surface made standing difficult for her.

Every instinct in her little body screamed, *Protect yourself! Do whatever it takes to keep yourself from falling.* And that's precisely what she did. She adjusted her position repeatedly and fought hard to stabilize herself and keep her feet from slipping. But the more she tried, the more she slipped, and the more she slipped, the harder she tried. Even when I put her in the safest place, in the position that gave me a better grip on her, she would not stand still. At that point, I whispered to her, "Just stand baby. I'm holding you, and I will not let you fall."

At that moment, the Holy Spirit whispered to me, "That's exactly what you have been doing: trying to hold yourself up."

If I wasn't there to hold my daughter up and she had stopped trying to stand, that would be giving up. But if she gave over control to me, to the one who is better able to hold her up, that is surrender. True surrender is to willingly hand control over to the One who will sustain us. It is admitting that without God, we can do nothing.

God our Father is committed to our success, and he will hold us up. Because of our relationship with Jesus Christ, we have the right to be called sons of God (John 1:12). Therefore, God's promise to the nation of Israel, his firstborn son, extends to us. God declares himself the helper of Israel, the helper of Abraham's descendants. He will hold us up with his mighty hand.

When we surrender, God unleashes unmatched power and unwavering commitment to our victory. Knowing this, would you be willing to surrender to God?

> *"When we surrender, God unleashes unmatched power and unwavering commitment to our victory."*

INVITATION

Humble yourselves, therefore, under God's mighty hand, that he may lift you up in due time. Cast all your anxiety on him because he cares for you.
— 1 Peter 5:6-7

The LORD makes firm the steps of the one who delights in him; though he may stumble, he will not fall, for the LORD upholds him with his hand.
— Psalm 37:23-24

So do not fear, for I am with you; do not be dismayed, for I am your God. I will strengthen you and help you; I will uphold you with my righteous right hand.
— Isaiah 41:10

Surely God is my help; the Lord is the one who sustains me. — Psalm 54:4

CALL TO ACTION

Take time alone with your thoughts. Get comfortable with the word surrender. Throw out the thought of surrender as a failure and replace it with the understanding that surrender is an act of wisdom and strategy. Accept that you are safer in God's hands than on your own.

PRAYER

Heavenly Father, I surrender my will and my way to you. I give up my constant fixing and my false sense of security. You are the one who sustains me. I trust you because you have promised that you will never leave me or forsake me. Amen.

REFLECTIONS

DAY TWO

Come

"Coming home." There is an unexplainable feeling we experience after a long, harsh day, returning to a place of comfort and safety. That moment of serenity is but a trickle of what it feels like to come to our Heavenly Father.

In my twenties, I left the safety of home to pursue a relationship that not only robbed me of my identity but also severed my relationship with my Heavenly Father. Looking back, I can see how my un-surrendered heart created a longing for something I thought I lacked. This caused me to remain in that relationship even when I felt degraded and undervalued. When it had cost me more than what I expected to gain, I still stayed. But when I sought my Heavenly Father, he told me, "You do not have to settle for less than what I have for you." Those words gave me the strength to break free from that relationship and come home.

Jesus told a similar story in Luke 15:11-32 about a man and his two sons. The younger of the two made an unusual request for his share in the father's estate. I suspect such a request was disrespectful and heartbreaking; nevertheless, his father divided all he had between the two sons. Soon after, the younger son gathered all his belongings and left the father's house. With this newfound freedom and the funds to support the lifestyle of his choice, the son did not restrain himself. The Bible says he went to "a distant country and squandered his wealth with wild living" Luke 15:13.

Sometimes, in our unwillingness to surrender to God, we can convince ourselves that we can do better apart from God. We are deceived into believing that the boundaries set by our Heavenly Father prevent us from having a rewarding, fulfilling, exciting life. Allowing ourselves to be drawn away from the protection and provision of God our Father can be devastating. When we become consumed by our desires and entangled by sin, we easily discard our priorities and values. We can become so trapped by shame and guilt that we struggle to relinquish control. But the Bible says when the son came to his senses, he realized that life was better in his father's house, so he returned home (Luke 15:17-20).

Even when sin has taken us where we never intended to go, God our Father shows us compassion. With the simple utterance of the words, "I have sinned against you," our Father welcomes us home, just like the prodigal son.

It doesn't matter what you have done or where you are coming from; just come.

> "It doesn't matter what you have done or where you are coming from; just come."

INVITATION

Come to me, all you who are weary and burdened, and I will give you rest. Take my yoke upon you and learn from me, for I am gentle and humble in heart, and you will find rest for your souls.
— Matthew 11:28-29

Let us therefore come boldly to the throne of grace, that we may obtain mercy, and find grace to help in time of need.
— Hebrews 4:16 KJV

If we confess our sins, he is faithful and just and will forgive us our sins and purify us from all unrighteousness.
— 1 John 1:9

CALL TO ACTION

Step into the throne room of grace, where Jesus sits at the right hand of God the Father. Sit at the feet of the Father and let him lavish his love on you. Surrender your heart to God, breathe in his peace, and breathe out the cares of this world. Be refreshed, restored, and revived.

PRAYER

Today, I come humbly to your throne of grace, O Lord, not asking anything except to be in your presence. To feel your embrace, to hear your voice, like a child running home from a harsh world, Lord, I come. Bruised, and broken, I come with my fears and failures, toils and trials; I have come to rest in your presence and experience your love. Amen.

REFLECTIONS

DAY THREE

Prized Possessions

Growing up in the Caribbean, we had an unwritten rule that prevented us from giving something to someone and then asking to have it back. This rule was meant mostly for tangible items, but it took on a different meaning when I became a parent. I had gifted my daughter to God at her birth, but by her teens, I had taken her back.

When my daughter was about fourteen years old, our relationship became a bit turbulent. To be fair, most of it was my doing—I was trying to mold her according to my own plans and expectations, not God's. Even though I had given her to God in the beginning, somewhere along the way, I had taken her back. Realizing this, I surrendered her to God once again. My approach to parenting changed, and our relationship improved. I was not just parenting my child; I was also parenting a child I had gifted to God.

In Genesis 22:1-18, God had quite an unusual request of Abraham. Abraham was one hundred years old, and his wife Sarah was ninety. It had been twenty-five years of trusting God before their promised son Isaac was born. To say that Isaac was Abraham's most prized possession would be an understatement. So, I can only imagine the sheer bewilderment Abraham experienced when God requested that he sacrifice Isaac.

Nevertheless, in an act of complete surrender, Abraham gathered all he needed for the sacrifice and headed for the mountain. Abraham was obedient even with his most prized possession. This act of surrender placed him in "right standing" with God and positioned future generations for God's favor and blessing.

In Genesis 22:16-18 God said, "Because you have obeyed me and have not withheld even your son, your only son, I swear by my own name that I will certainly bless you. I will multiply your descendants beyond number, like the stars in the sky and the sand on the seashore. Your descendants will conquer the cities of their enemies. And through your descendants all the nations of the earth will be blessed—all because you have obeyed me" (NLT).

Whatever the object of our affection is, holding on to it is the opposite of what God requires. We aren't equipped to bear sole responsibility for our prized possessions. Our best efforts to direct and secure what we love are limited in their returns and defenses; therefore, we must surrender them to God.

If we cannot surrender our prized possessions to God for him to use as he determines, then our prized possession is our god. Although we may never have to place our prized possessions on a physical altar like Abraham did, we must certainly give them to God.

> "Whatever the object of our affection is, holding on to it is the opposite of what God requires."

INVITATION

You shall have no other gods before me. You shall not make for yourself an image in the form of anything in heaven above or on the earth beneath or in the waters below. You shall not bow down to them or worship them; for I, the LORD your God, am a jealous God.
— Exodus 20:3-5b

Anyone who loves their father or mother more than me is not worthy of me; anyone who loves their son or daughter more than me is not worthy of me.
— Matthew 10:37

Honor the LORD with your wealth, with the firstfruits of all your crops; then your barns will be filled to overflowing, and your vats will brim over with new wine. — Proverbs 3:9-10

"Cursed is the cheat who has an acceptable male in his flock and vows to give it, but then sacrifices a blemished animal to the Lord. For I am a great king," says the LORD Almighty, "and my name is to be feared among the nations."
— Malachi 1:14

CALL TO ACTION

Ask the Holy Spirit to search your heart and show you your most prized possessions. Now, step into the throne room of God and lay them at his feet. Whether it is your children, wealth, career, education, spouse, beauty, or fame, surrender it all to God.

PRAYER

I come to you, Lord, bringing my most prized possessions, the things I hold dear. Forgive me for withholding what you have requested. I trust you and know that you can better care for what I care most about. You are all-knowing and all-powerful; my prized possessions are safe in your hands. Amen.

REFLECTIONS

DAY FOUR

Past Hurts

DEVOTION

Leaving the past in the past is as difficult as it is necessary.

There is a delicate balance between allowing yourself time to heal from hurt and trauma and letting go. The healing process will differ for everyone, and the help required will vary—from finding a safe space to sharing or needing professional intervention. No matter how traumatic an event or how deeply hurt we may have been, at some point, we have to surrender our pain to God.

I was in my early teens when my father moved to another country for work. This was supposed to be a temporary arrangement, however, by my late teen years, he had completely severed all communication with us. For many years, I held on to the hurt and anger that came from that abandonment, not realizing that my un-surrendered past was influencing my present. When I surrendered the past—which I could neither control nor change—I permitted God to intervene on our behalf. My father never returned home, but in time I was free to move forward without the residue of the past.

Esau knew the pain of a family member's betrayal. Esau and Jacob were twin brothers. Their relationship was rivalrous from its inception. As they grew, it got more complicated, with each brother vying for the firstborn blessing. In Genesis 27, Jacob, the younger of the two, known

13

for his trickery, enacted the ultimate betrayal. He skillfully impersonated his brother and misled their father into giving him his brother's blessing.

Esau was devastated and pleaded with his father for a blessing too. So, Isaac whipped up a somewhat secondary blessing, a remnant of the original blessing for Esau. But its full realization was predicated on Esau freeing himself of Jacob. For Esau to truly experience freedom, he had to let go of this seemingly unforgivable act. The quality of his life was conditioned on him growing restless and throwing his brother's yoke off his neck.

In the years to come, Esau learned to surrender his past hurts. When the brothers reunited for the first time since the betrayal, "Esau ran to meet Jacob and embraced him; he threw his arms around his neck and kissed him. And they wept" (Genesis 33:4).

We are not strangers to betrayal, heartbreak, and disappointments. If we do not let go of our past, we are yoked to the person and the pain and we carry the weight of betrayal into the future. Like Esau, our ability to move forward in victory is tied to our willingness to surrender our past.

> *"Our ability to move forward in victory is tied to our willingness to surrender our past."*

INVITATION

Forget the former things; do not dwell on the past. — Isaiah 43:18

Let your eyes look straight ahead; fix your gaze directly before you. Give careful thought to the paths for your feet and be steadfast in all your ways.
— Proverbs 4:25-26

Do not take revenge, my dear friends, but leave room for God's wrath, for it is written: "It is mine to avenge; I will repay," says the Lord.
— Romans 12:19

There is a time for everything, and a season for every activity under the heavens: a time to weep and a time to laugh, a time to mourn and a time to dance.
— Ecclesiastes 3:1, 4

CALL TO ACTION

For a brief moment, recall the event that has caused you pain and accept that it happened. Mourn your losses, accept what has changed, and resolve to move forward. Close your eyes, picture yourself in the presence of God, and give him everything connected to that event. Trust God and receive his peace and joy.

PRAYER

Lord Jesus, today I surrender my past to you, every experience and hurt that has made me who I am. I surrender the pain of betrayal, broken promises, and disappointments that have weighed me down. I unburden myself, I break the yoke off of my neck, and I receive your joy, peace, and freedom. Amen.

REFLECTIONS

Time and Talent

DEVOTION

Time is fleeting and without recall. It is the most precious human commodity, yet it is the most wasted. With the advancement of technology, we can spend hours engaged and entertained but do nothing of value or purpose.

A few years back, I attended a presentation on the importance of prioritizing. To convey this valuable lesson, the presenter used two large jars, a few rocks, pebbles, and sand. He filled one jar with the smaller items first, the sand and the pebbles, but was unable to add all the rocks because the jar was full. In the second jar, he added the rocks, pebbles, and, finally, the sand. Surprisingly, when the large items were added first, there was enough room to fit the smaller items into the jar. This concept holds true in our lives: How we prioritize our time and, subsequently, our talents will determine how much we can fit into our life span.

King Hezekiah learned about priorities on his deathbed. In 2 Kings 20, we are allowed access to a private conversation between Hezekiah and the prophet Isaiah. Hezekiah was sick, and the prophet brought him a word from the Lord. The king was instructed to put his house in order in preparation for his death. On hearing the instruction, the king prayed to the Lord, "Remember, LORD, how I have walked before you faithfully and with wholehearted devotion and have done what is good in your eyes" (v. 3).

In these words, Hezekiah replayed his life before God and gave an account of his devotion to the Lord's work. He showed the results of his time and talent. Then something rare happened: God amended his decision; the prophet reported that God had heard the king's prayer and seen his tears, and he would heal him and add fifteen years to his life (2 Kings 20:4-6).

King Hezekiah's request was granted because he invested his time and talent well. God, in his sovereignty, determined that his work would benefit more from Hezekiah's presence on the earth. We may not all have the opportunity to reason with God, and an abbreviated lifespan does not mean we could not prove our usefulness on the earth. However, we will all have to give an account for how we invested the time and talents we were given. When we surrender our time and talents to God, we make God our number one priority. We seek him first and we invest our time and talent for his glory.

If God required your life today, and you had the opportunity to plead your case, could you convince him to give you more years based on how you used your time?

> "Time is fleeting and without recall. It is
> the most precious human commodity,
> yet it is the most wasted."

INVITATION

Teach us to number our days, that we may gain a heart of wisdom.
— Psalm 90:12

Be very careful, then, how you live—not as unwise but as wise, making the most of every opportunity, because the days are evil.
— Ephesians 5:15-16

Show me, LORD, my life's end and the number of my days; let me know how fleeting my life is. You have made my days a mere handbreadth; the span of my years is as nothing before you. Everyone is but a breath, even those who seem secure.
— Psalms 39:4-5

Now listen, you who say, "Today or tomorrow we will go to this or that city, spend a year there, carry on business and make money." Why, you do not even know what will happen tomorrow. What is your life? You are a mist that appears for a little while and then vanishes.
— James 4:13-14

ACTION

Take inventory of how you spend time and talents. Be intentional about setting aside time for God and loved ones. Set priorities, God first. Include prayer, reading the Word, and serving. Set goals and be purposeful. Use your unique knowledge and skills to strengthen God's kingdom. Ask the Holy Spirit to reveal your purpose.

PRAYER

Today, I surrender my time and talents to you, Lord. I will give you the most productive, most effective, most energetic time of my day. I will use the gifts and skills you have given me for your glory. In my waking awake, un-tired times, I will seek you in prayer and praise. I will incline my heart to hear from you and do your will. Amen.

REFLECTIONS

_____

_____

_____

_____

_____

DAY SIX

Needs and Desires

Sometimes our needs are overwhelming, and our desires consuming. What can we do when we have done all we know to do? We surrender.

A few years back, my husband and I set aside work to attend Bible college. We had planned and saved and were ready to pursue the call of God. Unfortunately, things did not go as planned. Within the first few months, we faced every emergency imaginable and spent every dime we had saved. We had a choice to make: trust God and surrender our needs or discard our pursuit.

The Israelites faced a similar crisis. After four hundred and forty years of slavery in Egypt, God delivered the Israelites. So great was their deliverance that they sang of his great power and might (Exodus 14-15). However, by Exodus 16, they wished they had died at the Lord's hand in Egypt. Why?

Because they were hungry.

Our needs can become so compelling that, if we are not cautious, we can give up the best of ourselves, forfeit our destiny, or forego our freedom to fulfill them. If we allow our needs and desires to become what propels us, we will unconsciously become enslaved to them. God does not want us to make our jobs, careers, and businesses the source by which our needs are met. We must remember that God is our Father, and he is our only source. Anything apart from God is a channel that he uses to meet our needs.

In Bible college, God used a guest lecturer and an impromptu fundraiser to meet our needs. For the Israelites, God rained meat and manna from heaven and quenched their thirst with water from a rock. He kept their clothes from wearing out and their feet from swelling. And for the generation that trusted him, he brought them into the Promised Land. In Deuteronomy 8:10-18, God reminded them that when they were full of good food and had built their fine houses, they should not forget the One who gave them the power to get what they needed.

Surrendered needs and desires unburden us and bring us back into alignment with God's original design. We can trust God to meet all our needs, whether food, clothing, safety, love, esteem, or purpose. God's willingness to grant us the desires of our hearts is first tied to our readiness to delight ourselves (find contentment, joy, and fulfillment) in him. When God can trust that we are truly satisfied with him alone, there is no limit to what he will grant us.

> *"Surrendered needs and desires unburden us and bring us back into alignment with God's original design."*

INVITATION

So do not worry, saying, "What shall we eat?" or "What shall we drink?" or "What shall we wear?" For the pagans run after all these things, and your heavenly Father knows that you need them. But seek first his kingdom and his righteousness, and all these things will be given to you as well.
— Matthew 6:31-33

And my God will meet all your needs according to the riches of his glory in Christ Jesus. — Philippians 4:19

Take delight in the Lord, and he will give you the desires of your heart.
— Psalms 37:4

Do not be anxious about anything, but in every situation, by prayer and petition, with thanksgiving, present your requests to God.
— Philippians 4:6

ACTION

Ask the Holy Spirit to reveal your needs to you; do not focus on what you want. Write what the Holy Spirit says you need and make that a part of your daily prayer. Trust God to meet those needs.

PRAYER

Heavenly Father, thank you for providing me with every good thing. You alone are my source. I surrender to you every need and desire, and I trust that you will never put me to shame. You are a good Father who delights in taking care of your children. Lord, I thank you for your faithfulness. Amen.

REFLECTIONS

DAY SEVEN

My Life

DEVOTION

All to Jesus I surrender, all to him I freely give.

Most of us have heard or sung these words dozens of times. But surely a surrendered life is more than lyrics or a statement. True surrender is visible in our actions. A truly surrendered life does not need an explanation or understanding to comply.

One morning I woke up early to cry out to God. I felt like my life was spiraling. So much of what I was believing God for was not coming through; in fact, things seemed to be getting worse. I was tired, burdened, and overwhelmed, and I wanted God to reassure me that he had a way out.

After a few minutes of pouring out my heart, I heard the Lord say, "I hear you, but I have something to tell you." So I quieted myself and listened.

I don't think God ever addressed my prayer. But, by the time he had finished speaking, my entire state had changed, though my circumstances did not. I no longer felt broken and beaten down—I was strengthened and revived, and what seemed like pressing needs faded. I simply surrendered.

A surrendered life is not easy, but it's simple. When we are truly surrendered to God, we are no longer driven by our will. Instead, we allow God to do with us, whatever pleases him. We become fully convinced that all things work together for the good of those who are called to his purpose.

Luke 22:42 gives us a vivid description of a surrendered life. Jesus, faced with the reality of his suffering and death, being fully aware of the cost, fell to the ground and poured his heart out to God. "Father, if you are willing, take this cup from me; yet not my will, but yours be done." Jesus made a decision: Regardless of the pain and suffering ahead, he would surrender his life. He knew that he could trust the Father for a better outcome, far more than what he would receive being led by his will.

Every day, we face the same decision: surrender to God or do it our way. Whatever your decision, know that a surrendered life will always exceed your expectations. God can and will do more than you can ask or imagine. So, give up control and trust that God knows best and is in the best position to sustain us.

In total surrender, we understand that if we make a wise investment and it does not work out, it's the Lord's to redeem. If we train our children in the way they should go and they make poor decisions, they are the Lord's to restore. If we take the best care of ourselves and still fall ill, our bodies are the Lord's to recover. If we give and what is given back to us falls short, God will repay. If we love like Christ and we're betrayed, vengeance is the Lord's. If we lose our life for Christ, eternity is ours to gain; in reality, we never lose. "For to me, to live is Christ and to die is gain" (Philippians 1:21).

> *"Every day, we face the same decision:*
> *surrender to God or do it our way."*

INVITATION

Trust in the LORD with all your heart and lean not on your own understanding; in all your ways submit to him, and he will make your paths straight.
— Proverbs 3:5-6

Therefore, I urge you, brothers and sisters, in view of God's mercy, to offer your bodies as a living sacrifice, holy and pleasing to God—this is your true and

proper worship. Do not conform to the pattern of this world, but be transformed by the renewing of your mind. Then you will be able to test and approve what God's will is—his good, pleasing and perfect will.
— Romans 12:1-2

Do not offer any part of yourself to sin as an instrument of wickedness, but rather offer yourselves to God as those who have been brought from death to life; and offer every part of yourself to him as an instrument of righteousness.
— Romans 6:13

I eagerly expect and hope that I will in no way be ashamed, but will have sufficient courage so that now as always Christ will be exalted in my body, whether by life or by death.
— Philippians 1:20

CALL TO ACTION

Sit quietly and think about the statement, "I surrender my life." Let your thoughts move beyond the words. Foresee the daily actions that demonstrate a surrendered life. Should you find yourself overwhelmed, anxious, or worried, recall the areas we surrendered over the past few days and repeat them.

PRAYER

Lord, I surrender my life to you. I know that you are my loving, all-knowing, almighty Father who promises never to leave or forsake me. Like clay in the hands of the potter, my life is in your hands—mold me and make me what you want me to be. May my life bring you glory. Amen.

REFLECTIONS

FINAL REFLECTIONS

ACKNOWLEDGMENTS

First and foremost, I want to thank God, my Heavenly Father, for his unconditional love that saved me. I thank God for revelation, inspiration, and trusting me with his Word.

To my husband, Gary Pelotshweu, thank you for your unwavering support and love. Your belief in me and willingness to see my God's will be done is the force that propels me.

To my children, Lisa, TJ, and Zoe, thank you for unlocking a part of my heart that I didn't know existed.

To my mom, Jacqueline, thank you for your selfless giving and sacrifice.

To my siblings, Soneya, Angela, Msiba, OJ, and Akesia, thank you for your continuous support, honesty, and love.

To my parents by marriage, Lekoko (may his soul rest in peace) and Deborah Phindi Pelotshweu, thank you for your example of a life surrendered to God.

To my church family and my friends, thank you for believing in me, and for the opportunity to learn and teach the Word of God. Thank you for being a safe place in difficult times.

Last but certainly not least, thank you to VanDunk Edits for your professionalism and detailed editorial work.

This book would not have been possible without your love, support, and encouragement.

Stacy Pelotshweu
The pen of a ready writer

ABOUT THE AUTHOR

Stacy Pelotshweu was born and raised in Guyana, a vibrant country located in the northern region of South America. Her upbringing instilled in her a strong sense of community and a passion for helping others.

In her early twenties, Stacy embarked on a new chapter in her life by moving to Botswana, a country in southern Africa. There, she married and started a family, welcoming three beautiful Afro-Caribbean children into the world.

Stacy's commitment to education is evident in her academic achievements. She holds a Diploma in Advanced Children and Family Ministry from Christ for the Nations Bible College in Dallas, Texas, and a Bachelor's Degree in Business Administration from Botswana Open University. This combination of theological and business knowledge equips her to effectively serve both the spiritual and practical needs of individuals and families. Stacy's passion for serving others has manifested in her dedicated work within the church. She has served as both a Women's Ministry Director and a Children's Ministry Leader, guiding and inspiring others through her faith-based leadership.

As a speaker and teacher, Stacy has a gift for communicating her message with clarity and conviction. She has a deep understanding of the importance of faith in guiding individuals to their full potential. She believes in the transformative power of the Gospel to uplift and empower people from all walks of life. Stacy's unwavering commitment to service extends beyond the church walls. She is a devoted child of God and a Kingdom Citizen, actively seeking to make a difference in the world.

Stacy's life is a testament to the power of faith, dedication, and a genuine desire to serve others. She has woven together her personal experiences, educational pursuits, and spiritual convictions to create a life filled with purpose. Her journey has taken her across continents, but her commitment to serving others has remained constant. She has embraced challenges and opportunities with grace and resilience, leaving a lasting impact on those she encounters.

www.ingramcontent.com/pod-product-compliance
Lightning Source LLC
Chambersburg PA
CBHW022344040426
42449CB00006B/711